TESLA
MODEL S
BY EMILY ROSE OACHS

BELLWETHER MEDIA • MINNEAPOLIS, MN

Are you ready to take it to the extreme?
Torque books thrust you into the action-packed world
of sports, vehicles, mystery, and adventure. These books
may include dirt, smoke, fire, and dangerous stunts.
WARNING: read at your own risk.

This edition first published in 2018 by Bellwether Media, Inc.

No part of this publication may be reproduced in whole or in part without written permission of the publisher.
For information regarding permission, write to Bellwether Media, Inc., Attention: Permissions Department,
5357 Penn Avenue South, Minneapolis, MN 55419.

Library of Congress Cataloging-in-Publication Data

Names: Oachs, Emily Rose, author.
Title: Tesla Model S / by Emily Rose Oachs.
Description: Minneapolis, MN : Bellwether Media, Inc., 2018. | Series:
   Torque: Car Crazy | Includes bibliographical references and index. |
   Audience: Ages 7-12.
Identifiers: LCCN 2017031296 (print) | LCCN 2017036529 (ebook) | ISBN
   9781626177802 (hardcover : alk. paper) | ISBN 9781681034850 (ebook)
Subjects: LCSH: Tesla Model S–Juvenile literature.
Classification: LCC TL220 (ebook) | LCC TL220 .O23 2018 (print) | DDC
   629.22/93–dc23
LC record available at https://lccn.loc.gov/2017031296

Editor: Betsy Rathburn   Designer: Josh Brink

Printed in the United States of America, North Mankato, MN.

TABLE OF CONTENTS

QUIET RIDE

...ver walks toward his ...odel S. As he nears ...he door handles ... on their own. The ...ens the door and ...n. He presses his foot ...ake. The Model S is ... go!

door handle

The driver shifts the car into drive and presses another pedal. The Model S bolts forward.

The **electric motor** is nearly silent as the car gains speed. In seconds, it reaches 60 miles (97 kilometers) per hour. What a smooth, quiet ride!

electric motor

THE HISTORY OF TESLA

Martin Eberhard and Marc Tarpenning founded Tesla Motors in 2003. The two men were **entrepreneurs** who wanted to start a new project. They decided to make electric sports cars.

Martin Eberhard

A FAMOUS LEADER

ELON MUSK IS A FAMOUS INVENTOR AND BUSINESSMAN. HE WAS ONE OF THE FIRST PEOPLE TO GIVE MONEY TO TESLA MOTORS. LATER, HE BECAME CEO OF THE COMPANY.

Elon Musk

At that time, some people thought electric cars were less powerful than regular cars. Martin and Marc wanted to prove those people wrong.

Tesla's first car came out in 2008. It was called the Roadster. This car could **accelerate** quickly. It also had a longer **range** than other electric cars. It proved that electric cars can be as powerful as gas-powered sports cars!

Tesla Roadster

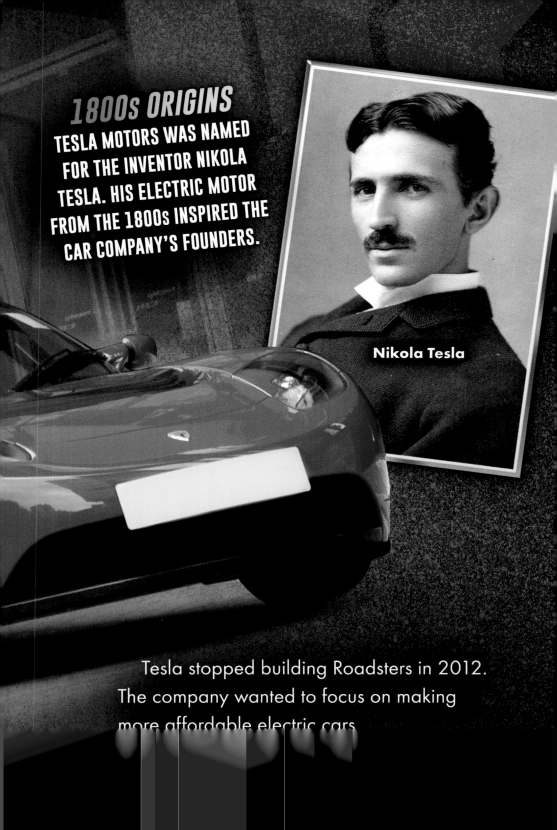

1800s ORIGINS

TESLA MOTORS WAS NAMED FOR THE INVENTOR NIKOLA TESLA. HIS ELECTRIC MOTOR FROM THE 1800s INSPIRED THE CAR COMPANY'S FOUNDERS.

Nikola Tesla

Tesla stopped building Roadsters in 2012. The company wanted to focus on making more affordable electric cars.

TESLA MODEL S

Tesla's next car was the Model S. This **sedan** came out in 2012. It matched the comfort and performance of the Roadster. But it had enough space for the whole family!

The Tesla Model S quickly drew attention after its release. It earned many awards. It also received a top safety rating!

Tesla Model S

TECHNOLOGY AND GEAR

The Tesla Model S runs completely on electricity. Its motor sits low and near the rear. A strong **battery** powers the motor. It allows the car to drive many miles between charges.

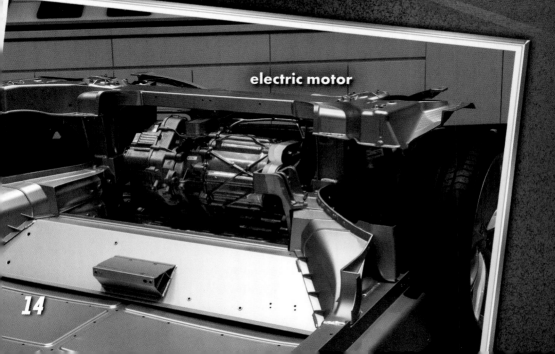

electric motor

The **sleek** body shape reduces **drag**. This helps the car travel as far as possible on a single battery charge.

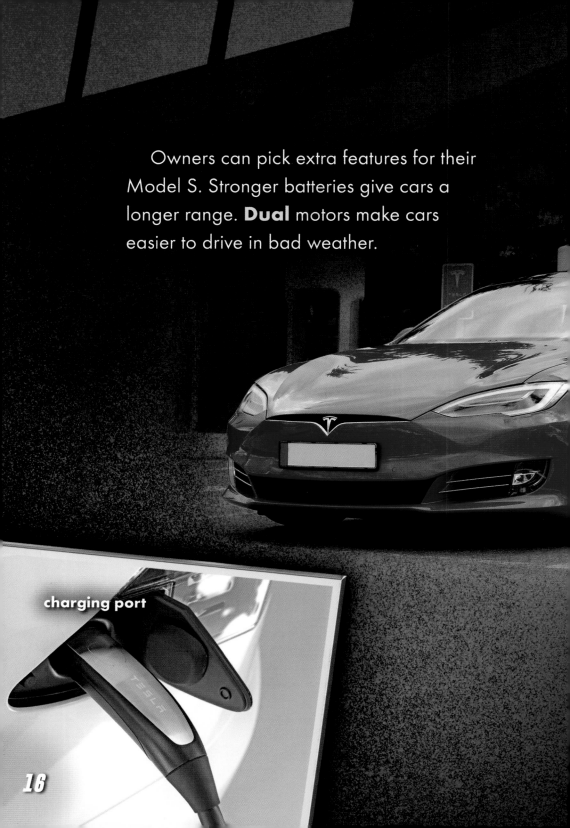

Owners can pick extra features for their Model S. Stronger batteries give cars a longer range. **Dual** motors make cars easier to drive in bad weather.

charging port

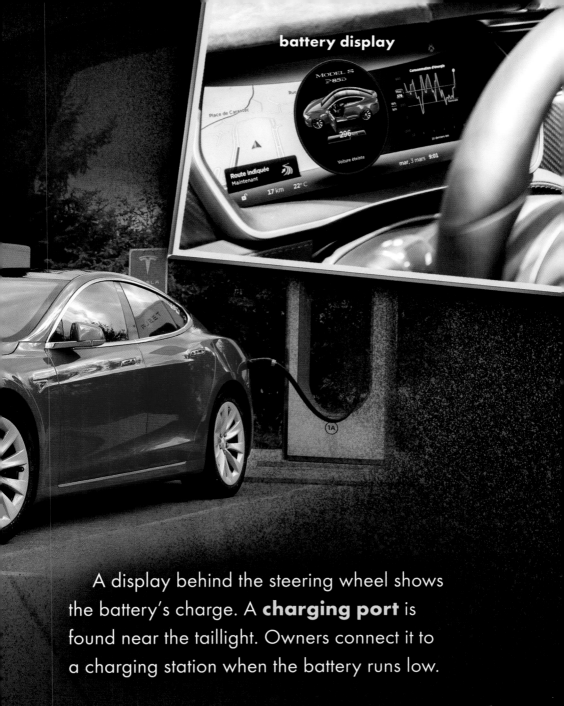

battery display

A display behind the steering wheel shows the battery's charge. A **charging port** is found near the taillight. Owners connect it to a charging station when the battery runs low.

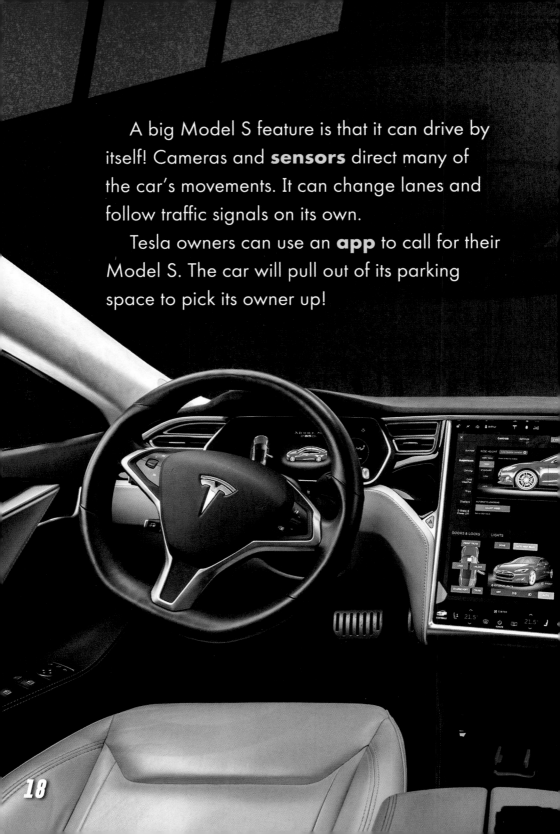

A big Model S feature is that it can drive by itself! Cameras and **sensors** direct many of the car's movements. It can change lanes and follow traffic signals on its own.

Tesla owners can use an **app** to call for their Model S. The car will pull out of its parking space to pick its owner up!

2017 TESLA MODEL S SPECIFICATIONS

CAR STYLE	SEDAN
MOTOR	ELECTRIC
TOP SPEED	155 MILES (249 KILOMETERS) PER HOUR
0 - 60 TIME	AS LITTLE AS 2.5 SECONDS
HORSEPOWER	STARTS AT 382 HP (285 KILOWATTS)
CURB WEIGHT	4,647 POUNDS (2,108 KILOGRAMS)
WIDTH	86.2 INCHES (219 CENTIMETERS)
LENGTH	196 INCHES (498 CENTIMETERS)
HEIGHT	56.5 INCHES (144 CENTIMETERS)
WHEEL SIZE	19 INCHES (48 CENTIMETERS)
COST	STARTS AT $69,500

TODAY AND THE FUTURE

The Model S is the leading electric car on the road. As technology improves, it may become even more popular.

Tesla continues to add new cars to its lineup. Electric cars may one day rule the road!

HOW TO SPOT A TESLA MODEL S

FLAT DOOR HANDLES

ANGLED HEADLIGHTS

CHARGING PORT

A NEW TESLA

IN 2016, TESLA INTRODUCED ITS MOST AFFORDABLE CAR TO DATE. MORE THAN 300,000 PEOPLE SIGNED UP TO BUY THE TESLA MODEL 3!

Tesla Model 3

GLOSSARY

accelerate—to increase in speed

app—a small, specialized program downloaded onto a smartphone or other mobile device

battery—a device that supplies machines with electricity

charging port—the opening that allows a charger to connect to an electric vehicle

drag—a force that slows the motion of a car

dual—two

electric motor—a machine that uses electricity to power a car

entrepreneurs—people who start or run a business

range—the distance an electric car can go before it needs to recharge

sedan—a car with a hard roof and four doors

sensors—devices that help a car respond to changes in driving conditions

sleek—smooth

TO LEARN MORE

AT THE LIBRARY

Diaz, Julio. *Tesla Model S*. Vero Beach, Fla.: Rourke Educational Media, 2016.

Doeden, Matt. *SpaceX and Tesla Motors Engineer Elon Musk*. Minneapolis, Minn.: Lerner Publications, 2015.

Hunter, Nick. *How Electric and Hybrid Cars Work*. New York, N.Y.: Gareth Stevens Publishing, 2014.

ON THE WEB

Learning more about the Tesla Model S is as easy as 1, 2, 3.

1. Go to www.factsurfer.com.

2. Enter "Tesla Model S" into the search box.

3. Click the "Surf" button and you will see a list of related web sites.

With factsurfer.com, finding more information is just a click away.

INDEX